Friends of God

The Discipleship Diary

_____

(Name)

A Friend of God

Friends of God

The Discipleship Diary

Author: Mikal Keefer
Chief Creative Officer: Joani Schultz
Senior Editor: Candace McMahan
Assistant Editor: Cherie Shifflett
Illustration and Design: Andy Towler

ISBN: 978-1-4707-5557-7
Printed in the USA.
10 9 8 7 6 5 4 3 2 1   27 26 25 24 23 22 21 20 19 18

What's Inside

Hello, Friend!

Welcome to *Friends of God: A Discipleship Experience*! You're about to set out on an adventure—an adventure of friendship with Jesus.

You'll risk taking Jesus at his word that he wants to be your friend.

That you can know his heart for you.

That discipleship is more than one long, demanding to-do list.

That Jesus is ready and able to transform you—from the inside out.

That's because Jesus-style discipleship is all about your heart, Jesus' heart, and drawing the two of you closer together. It's moving past head knowledge to heart knowledge.

That's why, through a dozen get-togethers with other disciples and some eye-opening adventures, we'll keep our focus on the heart.

Your heart. Jesus' heart. And the hearts of the disciples experiencing this journey alongside you.

You'll love this—because this is where the joy is. The peace. The purpose.

And the fun.

So buckle up. You're following Jesus, and you never quite know where he'll take you.

You're a Friend of God—and Friends Get Acquainted

Your friendships have at least one thing in common: At one time, you weren't friends.

There's a time even you and your best friend were strangers. But then you got acquainted, and something sparked. Something drew you together, and once you got to know each other...well, that was the start of a beautiful friendship.

It's the same with your friendship with God.

Almost the same, anyway.

The truth is that God has always known you. Always known everything about you. And always loved you.

But you *haven't* always known God.

And it's possible that when others first told you about God, they muddled the message. Maybe they told you he was a stern taskmaster who watched to see if he could catch you making a mistake. Or that he was distant, not interested in you at all.

In this session you'll take a fresh look at God. You'll clear away the clutter and see him for who he really is, maybe for the first time.

And you'll consider whether the two of you could become close friends.

He'd like that—but it's up to you, too.

Names of Jesus

- The Bread of Life
- The Light of the World
- The Gate for the Sheep
- The Good Shepherd
- The True Vine
- The Word
- The Lamb of God

"I no longer call you servants, because a servant does not know his master's business. Instead, I have called you friends, for everything that I learned from my Father I have made known to you."

—Jesus
(John 15:15, NIV)

Talk About This

What are the differences between a servant relationship and a close friendship?

Fill in this statement:

"A servant relationship is *does not know his masters business* , but a friendship is *someone who knows your business and shares life with you.*

Jot your thoughts:

Adventures in Discipleship

After each session, you'll invite Jesus to help you grow closer to him.

He's all for that. Just as he called his first batch of disciples his friends, he's saying the same thing to you. And he's eager for you to embrace and deepen that relationship with him.

You're on an adventure with Jesus—an adventure of friendship.

Here's the thing about adventures: You're never quite sure how they'll turn out.

But that's why they're so much fun, right?

You and a friend set off on an hour's hike in the forest, make a wrong turn at that oak tree, and two hours later you're taking in a stunning view you'd never have seen if you'd stayed on the predictable path.

The big tour of New York City you so carefully planned is shut down by an unexpected blizzard, and you end up sledding in Central Park instead. Big fun and a story you'll never tire of telling others.

Another truth about adventures: They aren't as much about what you're doing as who you're with. And though you'll do some of the adventures in this book with a group and some alone or with a friend, Jesus will always be along for the ride.

He loves this sort of thing: moving you just outside your comfort zone so you can see him more clearly and rely on him more fully.

That's what disciples do—and that's how you deepen your friendship with Jesus.

So before your next session, here are opportunities to embrace the adventure you're on with Jesus.

The Names of Jesus

While you were at the group get-together, you talked about the name of Jesus that was most meaningful to you.

Take a few minutes to dig into the other names of Jesus as well.

Read the Bible passage associated with each name; then ask Jesus to tell you what that name says about him...and what it means to you in your friendship with him.

Don't rush this. Consider one name and then go on your way, letting Jesus speak to you about himself throughout the rest of the day.

Circle back the next day to explore another name.

There's no hurry—you're deepening your friendship with Jesus as the two of you become better acquainted.

The Bread of Life (John 6:35)
Jesus, what does this name say about who you are...and why is this important in our friendship?

The Light of the World (John 8:12)
Jesus, what does this name say about who you are...and why is this important in our friendship?

The Gate for the Sheep (John 10:9)
Jesus, what does this name say about who you are...and why is this important in our friendship?

The Good Shepherd (John 10:11)
Jesus, what does this name say about who you are...and why is this important in our friendship?

The True Vine (John 15:1)
Jesus, what does this name say about who you are...and why is this important in our friendship?

The Word (John 1:1)
Jesus, what does this name say about who you are...and why is this important in our friendship?

The Lamb of God (John 1:29)
Jesus, what does this name say about who you are...and why is this important in our friendship?

Wonderful Counselor (Isaiah 9:6)
Jesus, what does this name say about who you are...and why is this important in our friendship?

Being a Friend of God

Disciples are friends of Jesus, good friends. But it's tough to wholeheartedly follow someone you don't know or trust.

So pause to consider where your friendship with Jesus stands.

Because the word *friend* covers a lot of ground.

You might call a childhood buddy a friend even though you haven't talked in years. Or you might use the word to describe someone you see often, who knows everything about you including, you know, *that* thing.

Do this: Place a small cross in the space below that best describes the current status of your friendship with Jesus. Not where you think your friendship *should* be, but where it actually *is*.

It's okay if the two of you aren't as close as you'd like to be. You're moving in that direction, and friendships take time to grow and deepen.

Place a cross in one of the spaces now.

Stranger

You talk about the weather, but not about anything personal. A familiar face on the bus or at the gym, someone who you might not even know by name.

Acquaintance

You're getting to know each other, sharing some information and opinions—but only safe ones. You aren't sure you can trust this person.

Friend

There's trust now, and you're able to relax more. Conversations feel natural and flow easily. You care what this person thinks of you and care deeply about the person's welfare.

Good Friend

Your relationship has survived disagreements, and you've been there for each other through good times and tough times. You're not going anywhere; you're committed.

Best Friend

This is who you call when you need a lifeline. You can't imagine your life without this person in it, and the feeling is mutual.

Talk About It

Jesus is all-in when it comes to you.

He's committed to you right now—just as you are—even if you're not all that sure about him.

So when you take a next step toward him, growing as a disciple and friend, he is hugely happy.

A question for the two of you to talk about: What, if anything, is in the way of your friendship becoming even deeper? What will it take to overcome that obstacle?

Ask the question; then listen for whatever Jesus might tell you. Jot what you hear below. Jot your thoughts about the question, too.

Let's Talk About Your Name

Before Session 2, meet with a few friends to do what you did during the first session: Talk about your names.

Call or visit three friends and ask about their names. You might contact family members, buddies, neighbors, classmates—anyone you want to know better.

Hear their stories about their names; then ask follow-up questions to peel back additional layers of their stories:

- What about your middle name? What's the story there?

- How did you feel about your name when you were little?

- What awkward nicknames evolved from your name?

- If at some point your name changed, how did you feel about making that change?

Your friends will probably wonder why you're asking. Feel free to tell them about this *Friends of God Discipleship Experience*; you may open the door to faith conversations.

This will be fun and informative. You'll get to know these three friends better, and that's a good thing.

And it's also a good thing to have fun. Friendships are fueled by fun and laughter—and as you draw closer to Jesus, you'll find yourself laughing with him, too.

And that's just as it should be for disciples!

You're a Friend of God— and Friends Get Even Better Acquainted

When friends *really* get to know each other, they see each other more clearly.

They move past assumptions to insight. They're well enough acquainted that they can talk about the truly important stuff: what they really think, what they truly believe, who they actually are.

Friendship with anyone follows a natural progression from stranger to acquaintance to an acquaintance you're getting to know better.

And it's the same with Jesus.

You've heard *about* Jesus, but perhaps you'll discover something new if you talk directly *with* him about what you've heard. If you check your assumptions and let him straighten out anything that's gotten wrinkled along the way.

To be a friend of God is to be a friend of Jesus. He said that himself: "The Father and I are one" (John 10:30). It's pretty clear that to know Jesus is to know God.

So let's nudge our friendship with Jesus forward by getting better acquainted with him. Let's tune out the distractions and focus on him.

Because that's what disciples do.

Clues About Jesus

See what you can understand about Jesus' heart and personality by looking closely at the object you selected from nature.

What clues about Jesus are captured in the item you hold?

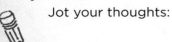

Jot your thoughts:

_____

_____

_____

_____

_____

_____

_____

_____

_____

_____

_____

"For ever since the world was created, people have seen the earth and sky. Through everything God made, they can clearly see his invisible qualities—his eternal power and divine nature. So they have no excuse for not knowing God."

(Romans 1:20)

A Message From Jesus

If your partner believes he or she may have heard something from Jesus for you, don't let it slip away. Jot down a word or two that captures the essence of what your partner shared.

And if you felt Jesus giving you a word, image, Bible verse, or other message for your partner, jot that down, too.

Hearing from Jesus matters—a lot. If you can recognize his voice in the midst of all the voices that fill your life, you're better able to follow him.

If Jesus gave you something to share with your partner, sum it up here.

Adventures in Discipleship

Before Session 3, embark on these discipleship-building adventures.

Dive in—you'll find that Jesus is always by your side as the two of you get better acquainted.

Creation Observation

During the group session, you focused on one tiny slice of nature.

Which means there's a lot of nature still out there reflecting God's "invisible qualities—his eternal power and divine nature." A lot of nature that's covered with Jesus' fingerprints and reflecting his heart for you.

So spend a bit of time outside.

You might take a hike in the mountains, stroll through your neighborhood, or spend half an hour sitting in your backyard—anywhere that gives you a chance to see the earth, the sky, and some of God's creation in between.

As you sit, ask Jesus to help you see things that reflect something true about him. Something that reveals his heart for you and creation.

Allow at least 30 minutes so you have a chance to slow down, focus, and open yourself to Jesus.

When you hear or see something you think might be from him, jot it down.

_____

_____

_____

_____

_____

_____

Why Are Jesus' Fingerprints All Over Nature?

Because he put them there.

If you thought Jesus first came on the scene as a baby in Bethlehem, you've missed a sizable chunk of his back story. Which means there are a few things you need to know about your friend as the two of you get better acquainted.

First, he was around at Creation and had a hand in it. Because—and this is even more important—Jesus is God.

That's who you're following as a disciple, as a friend.

If Jesus were on social media, the following Bible passages would be in the "About Me" section of his profile. Read them to get a sense of exactly who is calling you his friend.

Linger on each passage long enough to write your responses to the questions, too—it will help cement in you some powerful truths about the Jesus you follow.

***"God created everything through him, and nothing
was created except through him"*** (John 1:3).

Jesus isn't a supporting actor when it comes to knowing
God. Because Jesus *is* God, to know Jesus is to know God.
To follow Jesus is to follow God.

That's how powerful Jesus is—and he's calling you his friend.

*Other than Jesus, who's the most powerful person you
know? Write a name, and describe what makes that person
powerful. It could be the person's money, influence, or fame.*

*Whatever it is, how does that stack up against the power
of your friend Jesus?*

"For through him God created everything in the heavenly realms and on earth. He made the things we can see and the things we can't see—such as thrones, kingdoms, rulers, and authorities in the unseen world. Everything was created through him and for him. He existed before anything else, and he holds all creation together" (Colossians 1:16-17).

This is another reminder of Jesus' power during the process of creation.

But notice that last line—it's Jesus who "holds all creation together."

He's the glue that prevents it all from spinning into chaos, the power that holds all the moving parts and pieces in place. Which means he's not yet done with creation; he's still actively involved.

No wonder you can see his heart reflected in nature—it's his personal art project. And as part of his creation, as the masterpiece of his creation, your very being reflects who he is and what he values.

When you consider your body and emotions—where do you see God's "invisible qualities—his eternal power and divine nature" on display? Ask Jesus to help you see yourself clearly as you consider your answer.

"He came into the very world he created, but the world didn't recognize him" (John 1:10).

When Jesus arrived on earth, it wasn't with a sky-splitting bolt of lightning and peal of thunder that couldn't be ignored. True, a choir of angels announced his birth, but it was to a few wide-eyed shepherds on the outskirts of town who were told to look for him in a manger, of all places.

It was easy for people Jesus encountered to miss who he was because he didn't look the part.

So they didn't pay much attention to him. They didn't take the time to listen, to get to know him.

But when you *do* get to know Jesus, to understand his heart for you, everything changes.

You discover who he is and what he wants from you: friendship.

In what ways do you think you've not recognized Jesus for who he is? How are you getting better acquainted with him?

*"**This means that anyone who belongs to Christ has become a new person. The old life is gone; a new life has begun!**" (2 Corinthians 5:17).*

No question about it: Your friend Jesus is still in the creation business. Still leaving his fingerprints on nature.

Jesus transforms those of us who give themselves to him. He loves and accepts us as we are, but his love changes us. We begin doing the things he asks of us, not because of duty but because we want to please someone we deeply love.

Jesus isn't much interested in dusting you off and urging you to try harder to be a disciple. He knows you can't be completely faithful as you follow him (even his first disciples couldn't pull that one off!). He knows you can't grit your teeth and do all the right things.

So he's out to transform you.

As you grow closer to Jesus, as you follow him more closely, expect some things to change in you for the better.

That's Jesus at work.

In what ways has Jesus already transformed you? What changes, if any, do you sense happening in you because of your deepening friendship with Jesus?

If you'd like to see how Jesus shows up throughout the Bible—from the first page of Genesis to the last page of Revelation, explore the *Jesus-Centered Bible* from Group Publishing.

References to Jesus in the Old Testament are highlighted in blue ink, and throughout the Bible helpful inset boxes point toward Jesus.

Paying Ridiculous Attention to Jesus

Getting better acquainted with Jesus happens best when you pay attention to him. And not just when you pay attention, but when you pay *ridiculous* attention to him.

Part of hearing Jesus is realizing that he's still speaking to his followers, and not only through the Bible.

You can hear from Jesus in lots of ways.

Through the teaching of someone who's explaining the Bible to you. Through a caring word or the hug of a friend. Through pausing when you pray so you're listening as well as speaking.

It comes down to this: If you expect to hear from Jesus, you will. Not because that's the only time he's speaking, but because you're paying attention.

With that in mind, here are some ways you can pay attention to Jesus.

Place a check mark next to one of them, and in the next few days, act on it.

See what happens.

☐ **Fill in the gaps with Jesus.**

Gaps are those moments when you're between things. You've completed one task but aren't quite ready to begin the next one. Or you're stuck in line or stopped in traffic. During those moments, ask Jesus, "Is there anything you'd like to tell me?" And then listen.

☐ **Read the Bible, not for information but to build your friendship with Jesus.**

Instead of asking, "What happened in this passage?" ask "What are you showing me about yourself, Jesus?"

☐ **Slow down and look for Jesus in situations.**

If you're growing frustrated with someone, ask Jesus to help you see the situation through his eyes. When you're juggling enough tasks to qualify as a circus performer, pause and ask Jesus what's really important to do and what you can drop.

☐ **Ask Jesus to set your agenda.**

Rather than notifying Jesus of what you have in mind and asking him to bless it, tell him you're available and ask him what he has for you today. Then make that your priority.

☐ **Quiet your own voice.**

You're busy. You're distracted. And all that stuff gets in the way of hearing Jesus when he's speaking to you. So decide to intentionally silence yourself, and ask Jesus for his help in doing it.

☐ **Break out of your ruts.**

Take a new route to work or school. Take a cold-water-only shower. Write with your nondominant hand. Even simple things can shake you out of the predictable and safe and give you fresh eyes to see what Jesus is doing around you.

☐ **Pray in a way that you've never prayed before.**

Pray while kneeling. Pray out loud. Call a friend and pray together over the phone. The point: to pray in a way that fully engages you rather than allowing you to pray on autopilot. Pause often and see what response you might hear from Jesus.

☐ **Listen to the "Paying Ridiculous Attention to Jesus" podcast.**

You'll discover more practical ways to deepen your awareness of and friendship with Jesus.

Talk About Next Steps

Here's something for you and Jesus to discuss:

What's the next step in your friendship?

Remember where you placed the cross on the chart on page 12? Even if you plopped him down right next to you as a best friend, you can still get closer. Your friendship can still grow.

But how? What might he suggest?

Ask him—and pay attention to how he might be answering you. It probably won't be a text message with a specific request to get together for lunch. Instead, something will dawn on you during the next day or so: a thought, a glimmer of a thought that, once you consider it, sounds a lot like something Jesus would recommend.

When you hear it, do it. Disciples follow.

But first, ask.

And when you hear something, jot it down so you remember to follow up.

Nature Wander

This adventure puts you out in public in what might look like a "doing it alone" activity. But that's not the case—you're with Jesus.

Keep in mind that wandering through nature might include places like a local park, a farm, or a national wilderness area. Whatever is convenient works; God made it all.

Allow 30 minutes, and plan to pause three times as you wander.

During the first 10 minutes, ponder Jesus' extravagance—you're looking at a world filled with thousands of species. During the first 10 minutes, say to Jesus, "Show me your kindness toward me so I can thank you."

When your eye fixes on something specific in nature, ask Jesus how that small piece of creation communicates his kindness to you.

When you sense some clarity about his kindness, thank him.

During the second 10 minutes, ask Jesus this question as you wander: "What's an act of 'secret service' I can do right now?" Whatever surfaces—picking up trash, helping another walker, whatever—follow through with it immediately.

During the third 10 minutes, ask Jesus, "What do you love about me?" Remember, you're one of his creations, too. He's built into you all of the wonder that he's invested in the natural world you see around you.

Listen quietly. When you feel you've heard from Jesus, use some found objects to build a small altar to Jesus. Place the altar—a small mound of stones, a few branches arranged carefully—where they won't be easily disturbed but might be noticed.

When another walker notices, it might cause that person to hesitate, ask why someone built it, and glance around with fresh eyes to see Jesus in his handiwork.

Pause a moment by your altar to quietly worship Jesus.

Then go on your way.

You're a Friend of God— and Friends Know Each Other's Hearts

There's a huge difference between knowing facts about someone and knowing that person.

Think of a friend you know and love. Got that person in mind?

You might not know much about your friend's relatives or where your friend was born. Your friend's favorite ice cream topping might be a mystery to you. There are literally hundreds of facts you don't know about your friend.

But you know your friend's *heart*—and that's what makes you friends. That's what draws you together and cements your friendship.

The same is true with Jesus.

You won't find yourself passionate about following Jesus until you've moved past the facts and know his heart. That's when you shift from being a fan to a follower, from an admirer to a disciple.

In this session you'll focus further on discovering the heart of Jesus. It's something you've done in earlier sessions, and you'll do it again—because there's always more to Jesus than you expect.

Just when you think you've got him figured out, you find out otherwise.

Friends of God learn to live with surprises. They know that Jesus may call them to take a sudden left turn at any time, and that he's all about shaping their hearts to mirror his own.

One fundamental truth about Jesus is that he's not hiding anything—he wants to be known and known intimately. The more clearly you see him, the better you know him, the more passionately you'll follow him.

So let's clear away some of the underbrush that might be blocking your view of Jesus and his heavenly Father. Misunderstandings that might be keeping you from experiencing the heart of Jesus.

Seven Encounters with Jesus

1. Jesus and the Samaritan Woman (John 4:1-30)
2. Jesus and the Roman Officer (Matthew 8:5-13)
3. Jesus and the Gentile Woman (Matthew 15:21-28)
4. Jesus and the "Immoral" Woman (Luke 7:36-50)
5. Jesus and the Rich Young Man (Luke 18:18-30)
6. Jesus and Nicodemus (John 3:1-21)
7. Jesus, Lazarus, Mary, and Martha (John 11:1-44)

Notes

Adventures in Discipleship

 Before you meet for Session 4, here are some discipleship-building adventures to try.

Jesus' Heart

In the session with the whole group, you and some friends dug into one of Jesus' encounters. You explored the encounter to see what you could discover about Jesus' heart.

Do this: Read the rest of the stories.

As you read them, focus on how Jesus responded and why he may have done what he did and said what he said.

What is he revealing about his heart? about his values? about his feelings?

Tackle them one at a time, reading each story several times. Picture yourself standing next to Jesus, experiencing the story firsthand.

Then ask Jesus, "Help me see your heart here. I'm paying attention."

1. Jesus and the Samaritan Woman (John 4:1-30)
What is Jesus revealing about his heart in this encounter?

_____

_____

_____

2. Jesus and the Roman Officer (Matthew 8:5-13)
What is Jesus revealing about his heart in this encounter?

_____

_____

_____

3. Jesus and the Gentile Woman (Matthew 15:21-28)

What is Jesus revealing about his heart in this encounter?

4. Jesus and the "Immoral" Woman (Luke 7:36-50)

What is Jesus revealing about his heart in this encounter?

5. Jesus and the Rich Young Man (Luke 18:18-30)

What is Jesus revealing about his heart in this encounter?

6. Jesus and Nicodemus (John 3:1-21)

What is Jesus revealing about his heart in this encounter?

7. Jesus, Lazarus, Mary, and Martha (John 11:1-44)
What is Jesus revealing about his heart in this encounter?

_____

_____

_____

A Point to Ponder

A modern-day disciple named Brennan Manning wrote the following about the importance of getting to know Jesus...and what Jesus shows us about the heart of God:

> *"It must be noted that Jesus alone reveals who God is...We cannot deduce anything about Jesus from what we think we know about God; however, we must deduce everything about God from what we know about Jesus."*
>
> —Brennan Manning, *Ruthless Trust*

If this is true, in what ways is Jesus different from what you expect God to be, and why?

_____

_____

_____

_____

_____

_____

Who God Is

In the session with the whole group, you shared how you viewed God when you were young. Then you shared how you view God now and, if your view has changed, what prompted that change.

That's valuable information.

Why? Because your view of God says a lot about what you know of his heart.

So do this: Get together with a friend and do the experience again—this time on page 35. Explore your own story in more depth by talking about the experiences that have shaped your views of God.

See what you discover...and what misunderstandings you can put to rest.

If You See God as Something Other Than Benevolent...

God is loving and attentive. Really?

That's hard to accept when someone you love slowly wastes away because of a disease that God could heal but doesn't.

When the future you thought God had in store for you evaporates.

When it's your house that's hit by a tornado, hurricane, or fire.

How can you view God as loving when you aren't sure he has shown up for you? when you turn to look for Jesus and the comfort he promises and find...nothing?

Fair questions.

And questions God has heard before.

Two things: First, Jesus has never once turned away someone who came to him with a challenging, sincere question. If you're struggling to view God's heart as loving, say so. Tell him.

And second, God never promised to insulate people from hardship. The pain we let separate us from God is pain that

CRITICAL
God is a judge who grades our behavior, but he isn't involved in our lives.

DISTANT
God is completely removed from the details of our lives. God is a cosmic force and doesn't care about us.

AUTHORITARIAN
God is engaged with us but cares most about our obedience—being good people and following his rules.

BENEVOLENT
God is lovingly engaged with us and cares about us. He is a warm, inviting friend.

Place an X in the corner that best reflects how you viewed God when you were young. Then place your initial in the corner that reflects how you feel about God now.

If you shifted corners, why? Share some stories with your friend about what prompted the change.

he told us was coming. Pain he promises to walk through with us.

If you're to follow Jesus with anything approaching passion, if you're wanting to be a disciple, he's inviting you to make your way toward the Benevolent corner. Otherwise, you'll always hold God at arm's length.

If you have any hesitation about accepting God as both involved and loving, consider these Bible passages. Look for his heart in them.

"God is so rich in mercy, and he loved us so much, that even though we were dead because of our sins, he gave us life when he raised Christ from the dead. (It is only by God's grace that you have been saved!)" (Ephesians 2:4-5).

"The Lord isn't really being slow about his promise, as some people think. No, he is being patient for your sake. He does not want anyone to be destroyed, but wants everyone to repent."
(2 Peter 3:9)

"When we were utterly helpless, Christ came at just the right time and died for us sinners. Now, most people would not be willing to die for an upright person, though someone might perhaps be willing to die for a person who is especially good. But God showed his great love for us by sending Christ to die for us while we were still sinners" (Romans 5:6-8).

"For this is how God loved the world: He gave his one and only Son, so that everyone who believes in him will not perish but have eternal life. God sent his Son into the world not to judge the world, but to save the world through him.

There is no judgment against anyone who believes in him. But anyone who does not believe in him has already been judged for not believing in God's one and only Son" (John 3:16-18).

Talk About It

Disciples come to Jesus with their hard questions, knowing that their friend isn't afraid of fearless conversation.

So bring it on. Bring it all. Tell Jesus how you feel, and ask him to draw you closer to him as your friendship deepens.

Heart of Jesus

You and a group from your discipleship experience will go to a public spot and place Heart of Jesus Sticky Notes on or near things that remind you of the heart of Jesus.

For instance, you might be in a grocery store and see a parent being patient with an exhausted toddler. That patience might remind you of Jesus' patient heart toward you.

So give that parent a sticky note.

Or perhaps you're in the center court of a mall and see a fountain sending a sparkling spray of water skyward, reminding you of Jesus' extravagant love for you.

Stick a note to the side of the fountain.

The goal isn't to dispense the notes as quickly as possible; it's to create a space where Jesus can reveal himself to you.

Be open to Jesus directing your attention one way or the other.

Your group can wander about in pairs, but we recommend you travel to your destination together and then split up to take individual adventures.

You won't really be alone—Jesus is with you.

Spend no more than 30 minutes placing stickers. Then rendezvous and find a place to sit and talk (coffee shop, anyone?) as you discuss these questions:

- Where did you see the heart of Jesus? Share some stories.

- Why do you think the places you chose represent the heart of Jesus?

Now quickly decide some logistics with your group of four. Make decisions, take notes, and nail down the details below:

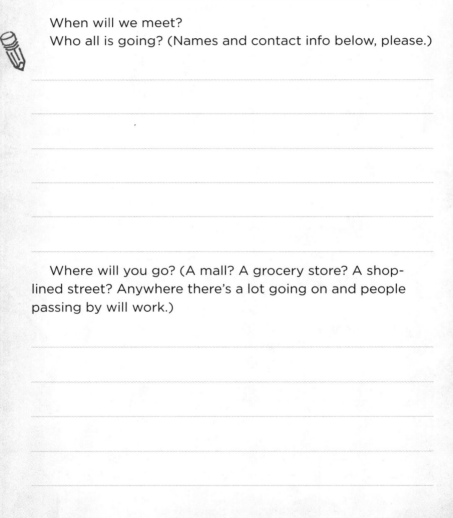

When will we meet?
Who all is going? (Names and contact info below, please.)

Where will you go? (A mall? A grocery store? A shop-lined street? Anywhere there's a lot going on and people passing by will work.)

And when you're back home and reflecting on your experience, ask Jesus this: "What did I discover about your heart, Jesus?"

You're a Friend of God—and Friends Both Talk and Listen

Not many friendships survive a constant diet of one-way conversations.

About the time you discover your new friend only wants to talk and doesn't ever listen...that's the same time you decide to move on and make a new friend.

Which means it's a marvel that God has been so very patient with us.

Because for many of us, that's what prayer often is: a brief time of telling God what we want, perhaps giving God some advice on how to fix something we think is broken, and then a quick amen.

There's no two-way conversation. No dialogue. No asking God how *his* day has gone so far.

Jesus modeled a far different sort of prayer. He made room for both talking and listening—paying attention to what God was telling him. It was a conversation between friends, and it's exactly how you can pray as well.

Because if you want a friendship with God, it's going to take both talking *and* listening, just like every other friendship you value.

In this session we'll try that sort of prayer on for size.

We think you'll love it.

And we're sure Jesus is a fan, too.

One-Way Communication Challenge

Here's room to draw what your partner is describing.

(If you weren't the one in your pair who drew, you can still use this page. Do the One-Way Communication Challenge with a friend!)

The Lord's Prayer

"Our Father in heaven, may your name be kept holy. May your Kingdom come soon. May your will be done on earth, as it is in heaven. Give us today the food we need, and forgive us our sins, as we have forgiven those who sin against us. And don't let us yield to temptation, but rescue us from the evil one" (Matthew 6:9-13).

Jesus' Words Prior to the Lord's Prayer

"When you pray, don't be like the hypocrites who love to pray publicly on street corners and in the synagogues where everyone can see them. I tell you the truth, that is all the reward they will ever get.

"But when you pray, go away by yourself, shut the door behind you, and pray to your Father in private. Then your Father, who sees everything, will reward you.

"When you pray, don't babble on and on as the Gentiles do. They think their prayers are answered merely by repeating their words again and again.

"Don't be like them, for your Father knows exactly what you need even before you ask him! Pray like this..." (Matthew 6:5-9).

"Taste and See" Notes

At any station you visit, there's a question for you to ask Jesus.

After you've asked the question, listen for his response and jot it down:

_____

_____

_____

_____

_____

_____

_____

_____

_____

_____

_____

_____

_____

_____

_____

_____

Dependent Prayer Notes

If Jesus gave your prayer partner any insights into you or your life, write them down here. Later, when you're alone with Jesus, talk with him about what your partner heard.

Adventures in Discipleship

Before Session 5, practice having conversations with your most fascinating friend, Jesus. Embark on these adventures…

Speed-Friending…With a Friend!

A discipleship skill that's seldom practiced is asking a question and then listening to the answer. This skill not only deepens your friendship with Jesus but also boosts all your other friendships!

During your last group get-together, you experimented with "speed-friending." You'll do the same thing again, but this time with just one other person.

So call a friend, promise to have some chips and salsa on hand, and when your friend arrives, go 10 rounds of speedy friendship-building.

Read a question aloud, and then take turns answering it. You'll each have two minutes to answer each question.

That's 10 questions…4 minutes per question…40 minutes altogether. Whew! That's a *lot* of listening—good thing you've got snacks to fortify yourselves!

Have fun. And when you've finished, discuss these questions with your partner:

- Which was easier for you: answering the questions or listening?

- Describe a friend who's a great listener. How does that quality affect your friendship?

- How do you know whether God is a good listener who hears your prayers?

10 Speed-Friending Questions

1. What have you dreamed about more than once?
2. Would you rather enroll in a math class or a cooking class? Why?
3. If you could fill a swimming pool with something other than water and then dive in, what would that something be?
4. What's your favorite kind of music? Why do you like it so much?
5. If you could meet any fictional character, who would you like to meet?
6. What's one of your favorite sounds?
7. Do you prefer winter or summer? Why?
8. If you could build a monument to any person you think deserves more recognition, whose monument would you build?
9. If you could watch Jesus perform one of the miracles in the Bible, which miracle would you like to see?
10. If you had to pick between them, would you rather visit the dentist or the doctor? Why?

The Prayer Chair

Pull two chairs into position for a comfortable conversation. Sit in one and imagine Jesus sitting in the other.

Picture the way he probably looked while on earth—a Jewish guy with a wide smile. Dark, weathered skin. Hands thick with calluses from his work as a carpenter. Dusty feet from a long walk that brought him to you.

Imagine his face—it's open and inviting. He's comfortable in his own skin and happy to see you. He's got a twinkle in his eye; he's been looking forward to this conversation.

His eyes are quick and understanding. And he's leaning forward, ready to hear and be heard.

Got all that in mind?

Now pray.

Eyes wide open, imagination fully engaged, have a conversation with the Jesus who's sitting across from you.

And make it a conversation, not a monologue. Pause often. Be willing to hear what he says.

Listen for a word, wait for an image to come to mind or even a snatch of a song or a Bible verse. But keep your focus on the chair and the man in it.

If you feel your focus beginning to fade, just wrap up. You can always invite Jesus for more conversation later. He's amazingly willing to reschedule.

When you've finished, make a few notes below. How did it go, and are you willing to do this again?

This activity is from *Help! How Do I Pray?* from Group Publishing. It's a guide to relational prayer that takes the guilt, intimidation, and boredom out of prayer by replacing how-to recipes and formulas with a focus on *who* you're praying to: Jesus!

An Adventurous Next Step!

Have you ever found yourself wanting to pray but feeling unsure of what to say?

Here's a thought: Ask Jesus what to pray about. Maybe he has something on the docket that you're not aware of.

Sitting down and saying, "Jesus, what do we need to talk about?" is respectful and conversational. And it's amazing how often Jesus has something he'd like to discuss with you.

After asking the question, simply quiet your mind and wait.

It's all part of having a childlike faith and a dependence on Jesus.

So rather than wait until you've accumulated an agenda to discuss, just ask Jesus: What would *you* like to talk about?

Then wait.

And go with it.

See where it takes you.

Of course, you'll be taking a risk. What if Jesus wants to dig into stuff you'd rather ignore? What if instead of working through your list of bless-mom-and-dad-help-the-needy he wants to explore your independent streak? or that addiction you've been hiding?

Giving Jesus control of the conversation is giving him permission to talk about what matters most.

Are you willing to do that? Are you willing to follow where he leads? It'll take some trust, but now that you're better acquainted with Jesus, perhaps you're ready to trust him this much.

Describe, in writing or drawing, where the discussion took you.

Talk About It

Ready for some risk?

Ask Jesus to tell you about...you.

About what he sees in you. About how he feels about you.

Friends do that, you know. They affirm and encourage each other. Ask Jesus to go first; then return the favor: Tell your Friend what you appreciate about him.

And whatever he has to say about you, write it below: It's something you won't want to forget.

Speed-Friending...With Jesus!

If this helped you draw closer to one friend, why not another? Jesus, for instance.

Here are three questions to explore with Jesus. Take 60 seconds to respond to each question; then quietly listen for 60 seconds to see what Jesus has to say to you.

- What do I want you to know today?

- Who needs your attention today, and why?

- What's important to do today—and what can sit awhile?

If you sensed a response from Jesus, if someone or something specific came to mind, do something about what you sensed. Get on it right away—you're following Jesus, and he may just have given you a specific assignment.

You're a Friend of God— and Friends Pay Attention to Each Other

One of the first things new Christians hear is that they should read the Bible.

So they do—or try to, anyway. They plow into Genesis, hold their own through Exodus, and start waving a white flag when they get to Leviticus.

And shortly thereafter they give up, relying instead on pastors and Christian writers to tell them what's in the Bible and what it all means.

Others persevere and become incredibly well-acquainted with the Bible, memorizing long passages and explaining historical and cultural context as they go. These are people who come to love the Bible, and it shows.

But the rest of us muddle along, hoping nobody will call on us when we're sitting through sermons, Bible studies, or youth group.

We've got a general idea what's going on, but the details are...fuzzy.

Could it be we're all missing the mark?

The point of opening the Bible isn't to master the material, to gather all the facts, and get all the details right. The point is to open up a message from a friend and to discover what that message says about God's heart.

The Bible's not a head thing; it's a heart thing.

The Bible gives us a front-row seat to watch God in action. To observe God interact with thousands of people throughout history. To feel him interact with you, now.

In this session we'll discover that the Bible's *real* purpose is to help us see and experience God's heart.

That its *real* purpose is to deepen our friendship with God. Starting now.

Three Encounters

Select one of these Jesus encounters; then read the passage and explore it with a partner. Ask "Why?" to see what you discover about Jesus' heart.

1. **Jesus and a Woman Caught in Adultery** (John 8:1-11)

2. **Jesus and a Man Born Blind** (John 9:1-12)

3. **Jesus Washes His Disciples' Feet** (John 13:1-17)

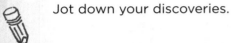

Jot down your discoveries.

Adventures in Discipleship

 Before your next get-together, explore these fun ways to grow in your friendship with God by paying closer attention to Jesus.

Asking "Why?"

In the group session, you and a partner explored an encounter Jesus had with a woman caught in adultery, a man born blind, or his dusty-footed disciples. You read the Bible's description of that encounter and repeatedly asked "Why?"—digging ever deeper into not just what Jesus did but *why* he might have done it.

And in the process you got a close look at Jesus' heart.

If you explored one encounter, that leaves two others for you to dig into, right?

But to do this, you'll need a partner—a friend who's not part of the *Friends of God Discipleship Experience.*

So call that friend and ask him or her to join you in this activity. Explain it won't take long—just 20 or 30 minutes—and it'll help you get comfortable with a new way to read the Bible.

Your friend can be a Christian—or not. What matters more is that your friend is the sort of person willing to help you cram for a final, catch a ride to the airport, or explore a new Bible-reading skill. It's the relationship that matters most here.

When the two of you get together, explain the benefits of asking "Why?" and then dive into the two encounters you didn't cover at the group meeting.

See what's revealed about Jesus' heart as you and your partner dive below the surface of Jesus' encounters by asking "Why?"

Capture your insights here:

_____

_____

_____

_____

When you've finished the activity, discuss this with
your partner:
*What did you discover about Jesus in this encounter that
wasn't apparent at first glance?*

And While You're at It...

Try asking "Why?" as you explore some of Jesus' other
encounters by yourself.

Here are five that may yield a fresh view of Jesus...

Mary Magdalene (Matthew 28:1-9)
*After asking "Why?" at least five times, what did you
discover about Jesus' heart?*

_____

_____

_____

_____

_____

_____

_____

Jesus and Two Dying Thieves (Luke 23:39-43)

After asking "Why?" at least five times, what did you discover about Jesus' heart?

Jesus and Pontius Pilate (Luke 23:1-6)

After asking "Why?" at least five times, what did you discover about Jesus' heart?

Jesus and Saul (Acts 9:1-9)

After asking "Why?" at least five times, what did you discover about Jesus' heart?

Jesus and Zacchaeus (Luke 19:1-9)

After asking "Why?" at least five times, what did you discover about Jesus' heart?

GOD'S BIG INSTRUCTION MANUAL
The Bible provides the rules and regulations we need to follow if we want to make God happy.

THE DUST-GATHERER
The Bible is a holy relic; it's around but doesn't have much to do with our everyday lives.

INTERESTING LITERATURE
The Bible is a collection of cool stories, but those moral lessons don't have any real authority in our lives.

GOD'S STORY OF LOVE
The Bible is God-inspired and tells the story of his love, a love that seeks to restore a friendship with us.

Place an X in the corner that best reflects how you viewed the Bible when you were young. Then place your initial in the corner that reflects how you feel about the Bible now. If you shifted corners, why? Tell some stories about what happened to prompt the change.

Revisiting the Four-Corners View of the Bible

In your get-together with the group, you and a partner talked about how you viewed the Bible when you were young. You then shared how you view the Bible now and, if your view has changed, what prompted that change.

Ask a friend—someone who's not a part of the *Friends of God Discipleship Experience*—to walk through that experience with you again.

Doing this a second time will help you explore your story in more depth and get to know your friend better.

So call your friend, and get together, using the chart on page 59 to see what you discover.

Lectio Divina

That's Latin for "sacred reading," by the way—and it's an ancient approach to reading the Bible.

It involves four steps:

Lectio—Select a passage—a chapter of the Bible, perhaps—and read it slowly. Don't worry about analyzing the meaning of the text. Just let your mind linger on individual words and phrases as you read. Let the passage sink in; consider reading it several times.

Meditatio—This is the meditation phase of the process. As you read, you're likely to find that you're drawn to one specific phrase or section of the passage. Zero in on it, reading it again and again, letting the words form a familiar pattern in your mind.

Oratio—Repeatedly recite aloud the phrase you were drawn to. You're creating a calm space in your mind and heart and letting the phrase God brought most vividly to your attention fill that space. It's prayer—only you're using God's words rather than your own.

Contemplatio—If you feel yourself drifting into meditation, go with it. Be silent, be still, and be in the presence of God.

Unless you happen to be a member of a monastic order, this may be a new approach to experiencing the Bible. It may feel awkward because you're setting aside the typical goal of studying a passage; instead, you're just letting it roll over and through you.

Lectio divina takes some practice, but it's worth trying.

My *Lectio Divina* Experience

Select a passage of Scripture and give this a try. If you don't have one in mind, here are several you might use: John 15:9; John 14:1; or John 4:13-14.

Even better, ask Jesus which passage *he'd* like you to explore.

When you've finished, jot down your thoughts about the experience. Describe how you felt, too.

This activity is from *Help! How Do I Read the Bible?* from Group Publishing. This little book is a breath of fresh air, providing practical, guilt-free, and relational ways to experience the Bible...and discover the heart of God.

Five-Whys Observations

Ask a friend to get together with you in a public place that's good for people-watching. The food court at a mall is a perfect location for reasons that will soon be obvious. Ditto a school cafeteria if you happen to spend time in one of those.

Describe how asking five "Why?" questions during the discipleship experience helped deepen a conversation—and a friendship.

Tell your friend you'd like him or her to help you sharpen that skill by joining you in asking "Why?" questions about people you see. For instance, why does that guy eating a burger have 45 tattoos? Why does the young woman sharing tacos with her three kids seem so calm in the midst of such chaos?

Ask one "Why?" question, and then follow it up with three or four more.

See where that leads, and be aware of this: Apart from asking the people you're observing, you really can't know for certain.

Maybe the man with tattoos has them to honor fallen comrades in arms. The woman is calm because she's a Jesus-follower or taking medication.

So do this: Risk approaching someone and actually asking him or her a question about what you've observed. Asked without judgment, questions can lead to remarkably cool conversations.

With people you see at the mall. And with Jesus.

By the way, just be sure to invite Jesus to accompany you as you both formulate questions and consider approaching others. Perhaps Jesus has you where you are for a reason.

You're a Friend of God—and That's About Relationship, Not Perfection and Performance

Maybe you think disciples should always *act* like disciples. They should be upright and honest; patient; consistently walking, talking advertisements for the transforming power of Jesus.

But have you taken a good look at Jesus' first disciples? The ones he handpicked and personally tutored?

They could be petty and jealous, unreliable and unlikely.

Flawed, one and all.

Yet Jesus didn't fire them because of their shortcomings. Instead, he zeroed in on those imperfections and invited his disciples to grow past them—with his help, of course.

So if you look at yourself and see a collection of random shortcomings with the occasional bright spot tucked in, here's the good news: You look like a disciple.

That's because perfection and performance aren't requirements for a disciple. A growing relationship with Jesus is what matters. A heart that's warm toward him and growing warmer.

Get that right, and the rest of the stuff, in time, will take care of itself as Jesus transforms you.

Dennis, the disciple featured in the film you saw, was far from perfect. Yet God used him. That's not because Dennis suddenly chose to be perfect; it's because God can use even a cracked clay vessel to carry living water to others.

God's like that. Skills beyond skills.
Power beyond power.
Love beyond love.

Adventures in Discipleship

During the group get-together, you were invited to see Dennis' story as a parable of sorts—a real-life story that might hold some insights into your life.

Taking time to answer the following five questions will help you mine Dennis' story for meaning in your own story of discipleship, your own friendship with Jesus.

And here's a sneak peek at what's coming the next time you get together with the whole group: You'll be asked what sort of insights surfaced as you answered these questions.

1. Ask yourself, "How do I see myself in this story?"

Before you answer, pause to ask Jesus to help you see connections. Wait for his direction, and then write what you sense is true.

2. **To what extent did you see God in control as Dennis' story unfolded?**

Lots of people say that God's in control, but do you think that's really true?

Dennis' life got messy—he was divorced, diagnosed with a chronic illness, and mistaken for a government agent. To what extent do you think God was behind those twists and turns in Dennis' story? And when you think of the messy and broken bits in your life, to what extent do you think God is behind those? Why do you answer as you do?

_____

_____

_____

_____

3. **What role did Dennis' brokenness play in his growing friendship with God?**

Do you think it helped or got in the way? And does the brokenness in your life help or hinder your deepening friendship with God?

_____

_____

_____

_____

_____

4. Why do you think Dennis still has so many questions?

Wouldn't you expect someone who's been as faithful as Dennis to have figured God out by now? What do you think it says that Dennis seems to have as many questions as answers? And if you were to ask Jesus a question and be certain of hearing a clear, complete answer, what would you ask him?

_____

_____

_____

_____

5. Using Dennis' story as an example, how would you describe the characteristics of a disciple?

Write some descriptive words below. Then decide which of them also describe you.

_____

_____

_____

_____

_____

Talk About It

Life's messy. That's no surprise to you and certainly no surprise to Jesus. But friends stick with each other through the messiness even if there seems to be no purpose to the messiness. Even if there's no happy ending for the marriage, no cure for the disease.

Dennis found that's true; Jesus stuck with him.

The question is this: Do you sense Jesus sticking with you through the messiness *you're* living through? Or do you feel you're gutting it out on your own?

Tell Jesus how you're feeling about the messiness and about how you do or don't see him walking alongside you.

Friends tell each other the truth. And since Jesus is your friend, he wants to hear the truth, as you see it, from you.

Movie Discipleship

Dig deeper into parables. How can a story hold truth for you even if the storyteller never intended that?

Do this: Call a couple of friends who aren't part of your discipleship experience group and explain you'd like them to join you for a movie, either at a theater or, better yet, your house.

Tell them it'll be an adventure. *That* should spark some interest.

If you decide to go to a theater, pick a time, and head to the theater together. Be sure to take your Glow Pen with you.

When you get to the box office, buy tickets to the next acceptably rated movie that's showing—even if you've never heard of the film. Even if you've heard of it and thought, "There's no way I'd sit through *that*."

Buy tickets, rustle up a jumbo bucket of popcorn to share, make your way to the theater, and settle into seats. Tell your friends you'd like them to look for two things in the film: where they see Jesus, and where they see themselves.

As the theater darkens, hoist your Glow Pen aloft, click it on, wave it around, and notice how heads turn in your direction. Click it off before anyone says anything, but notice how much attention just a bit of light draws.

That's what happens when you shine the light of Jesus in a dark world. It gets attention because even a little light has a huge impact.

That's you in the world when you're shining the light of Jesus. It matters.

If you opt to watch a movie at your place, darken the room, and do the same thing: Pull out your pen. Your friends will notice.

And be sure to pick a movie none of you have seen and watch it with the same two questions in mind: Where do you see Jesus, and where do you see yourself?

Afterward, share your thoughts. See what Jesus might teach you through your and your friends' observations.

You're a Friend of God— and Friends Take Risks With Each Other

Close friends move past playing it safe and take risks with each other.

They risk sharing secrets. Risk admitting they need help. Risk asking hard questions, knowing they'll get straight answers.

And they risk jumping into situations, not knowing exactly how everything will turn out. A road trip, maybe, or teaming up to do a home-repair project.

And that's one reason friends—close friends—laugh so freely together. Since they aren't worried about getting everything just so, they can relax. They care less about the destination and enjoy the ride.

That's the sort of friend you have in Jesus: one who's all about enjoying the ride.

If he'd wanted to make sure everything was "right," he'd have fired his first disciples and hired the Pharisees to follow him around. They were sticklers about being right and making sure all the rules were followed.

But Jesus cared more, then and now, about relationships than rules. He knows what we're finding out: If you know and love him, you'll just naturally want to please him. You'll want to be like him. You'll become a disciple because you've become a friend.

So take some risks with Jesus.

Risk following him, yes, but also risk relaxing with him.

Risk being his friend.

Experience: Taking Risks With Jesus

Describe Me
What words do you use to describe yourself?

What words does Jesus use to describe you?

Pick a Number
In what ways is Jesus inviting you out of your comfort zone?

Wear the Crown
How do you feel about being adopted into the family of a King?

Reveal Yourself to Me
What passage did Jesus highlight for you? What does he want you to know about himself or yourself?

Adventures in Discipleship

 Before your next get-together with your discipleship group, embark on any or all of the following adventures to explore your capacity for risk.

Taking Risks With Jesus

In the Bible lots of God's friends take risks. They risk life, limb, and livelihood...and those risks say something.

Read the following Bible passages, and after each one ask "Why?"

Why are these people taking these risks? And what do these accounts reveal about who Jesus is and what risks your friendship with him might mean for you?

Maybe these passages are familiar to you, and it's tempting to read them as history or to glean facts.

Go deeper. Ask Jesus to speak to you through these accounts...and listen to what he says.

1. Simon, James, and John Sign On as Disciples (Luke 5:1-11)
These fishermen walked away from their business—and income—to follow Jesus. Why? What's revealed here about their friendship with Jesus...and what might Jesus be saying to you in this passage?

2. John the Baptist Loses Influence (John 3:22-30)

John was the most dynamic spiritual leader for miles around until Jesus came on the scene. Choosing to play second fiddle to his cousin, Jesus, meant John was risking everything. Yet it's a risk John took. Why? And what might Jesus be saying to you?

3. Peter Gets Out of the Boat (Matthew 14:22-33)

A middle-of-the-night storm, a water-walking Jesus, and an invitation to join him by stepping out of the boat. Peter took the risk. Why? Ask Jesus if there are any boats you might need to step out of as well.

4. Joseph of Arimathea Goes Public (John 19:38-42)

This formerly secret disciple of Jesus asked Pilate for permission to claim Jesus' body from the cross. Why? What's Jesus' message for you in this passage?

---

5. Thomas Doubts Jesus (John 20:24-29)

Thomas wasn't sold on the whole resurrection thing—and risked saying so until Jesus showed up. Notice how the two interacted. What does that say about their friendship? What's Jesus showing you here?

6. Peter Speaks Up (Acts 2:22-24)

Telling the very people who had Jesus crucified that they're guilty of a crime? Dangerous stuff—but a risk Peter took. Why? What does it say about his friendship with Jesus...and what might Jesus reveal to you here?

_____

_____

_____

_____

_____

7. Stephen's First (Maybe)—and Last (Definitely)—Sermon
(Acts 6:8-15; 7:1, 51-59)

Stephen risked proclaiming the truth and was murdered for it. He knew the risk but took it anyway. Why? And what might telling the truth about Jesus mean for you? Ask Jesus to explore the answer to that question with you.

_____

_____

_____

_____

_____

Talk About It

Not everyone is wired the same when it comes to taking risks.

There are people who love risk-taking. Skydiving, bungee jumping, betting the bank on a new invention—bring it on. They love the adrenaline rush.

Plus there are spectacular stories to tell.

Other people care more about safety. They'd wear seatbelts in a recliner if safety gear came as standard equipment on furniture.

Most of us live somewhere in between.

And Jesus is a challenge for all of us.

In the big picture, there's no risk at all with Jesus—he's the Creator who has all the power he needs to usher those who follow him into heaven. Where will you be for eternity? If he's inviting you in, your spot on the guest list is guaranteed.

But between now and then: big risks.

Risk of conflict with a world that doesn't honor him. Risk of persecution. Risk of death.

Jesus told his first disciples, "If the world hates you, remember that it hated me first. The world would love you as one of its own if you belonged to it, but you are no longer part of the world. I chose you to come out of the world, so it hates you" (John 15:18-19).

Quite the recruitment speech.

Read John 15:18-26 and Matthew 10:34-39 aloud.

Then ask Jesus, "What risks are in front of me? How can the two of us take them together—and have a great time as friends as we're doing it?"

Singing in the Shower

The last time you were with the group, you sang "Jesus Loves Me" with the other disciples.

And you should know this: That simple song says it all. It says that you're loved. That the Bible is all about relationships. That you're in a dependent relationship with Jesus—he's powerful and you need him.

All in a song that most people quit singing when they were children.

Well, not you.

The next time you're in the shower, belt out that tune. Twice. Let it sink into your heart, and feel the reassurance and power of those clear, true words.

Extra points if you're in a shower at the gym.

Try This Taste

Call a friend and propose the following: You'll go to a restaurant, food truck, or taco stand where neither of you has been before.

Once there, you'll each order something you'd normally never order. Not something you know you hate, just something you've never tried before.

And when it shows up, you'll eat it. Maybe even sample each other's choices.

You're taking a risk, which means you may look back on this adventure as That Moment You Discovered You Like Sushi After All or perhaps as That Time You Were Really Grateful for the Breadsticks.

Either way, you're on an adventure, one whose outcome you can't predict.

While you're enjoying your meal (or...not), talk about this with your friend:

- How's this experience like or unlike other adventures in your life?

- What's a risk you've taken with a person or with God?

- Tell about a time you didn't take a risk but now you wish you had.

When you get home, ask Jesus what this experience can teach you about taking risks with him. Write down your thoughts and insights.

You're a Friend of God— and Friends Abide With Each Other

Abiding: deciding to stick with and be nurtured by someone.

It's what friends do, and when you're a friend of Jesus, it's *especially* what you do. That's because Jesus says if you expect to grow as his disciple and live in a way that shows you know him, you'll need his help.

And the only way to get that help is to remain in relationship with him.

And not just any relationship—a *dependent* relationship.

Many people aren't fans of depending on others—not even on Jesus. We like to think of ourselves as strong and self-reliant.

We'd rather give help than get it.

But that's not how it works for disciples. We're in the process of being transformed and bearing fruit that shows we're with Jesus. And all of that—the transformation and the ability to grow authentic fruit—depends on our staying connected to him.

Jesus uses the image of a branch being connected to a vine. Separate the branch from the vine, and the branch withers.

But if it stays connected? That's when it blossoms extravagantly and hangs heavy with fruit.

So what do you want to be? A dead branch...or a fruit factory?

The choice is yours.

Generosity Experience

To craft your generosity adventure...

- Work together as a group.
- Do a project outside this room.
- Be back in 20 minutes.

Adventures in Discipleship

 Before your next get-together with the discipleship group, dive into these discipleship-building adventures.

Dependence

Jesus said this:

> *"Yes, I am the vine; you are the branches. Those who remain in me, and I in them, will produce much fruit. For apart from me you can do nothing."*
>
> (John 15:5)

Do you see Jesus' words as empowering...or the opposite? Why?

Jot down your thoughts and feelings:

_____

_____

_____

_____

_____

_____

Decide to Abide

More than once Jesus talked with someone who listened but then turned and walked away.

And perhaps even more heartbreaking were those close to Jesus, those who'd stood with him and seen his miracles, who also turned away.

They were disciples who didn't stick, who didn't abide.

The Bible talks a lot about abiding—what it means and what it takes.

Read these passages and ask Jesus what he wants you to see in each passage. Jot down how you feel and what you hear.

"And now, just as you accepted Christ Jesus as your Lord, you must continue to follow him. Let your roots grow down into him, and let your lives be built on him. Then your faith will grow strong in the truth you were taught, and you will overflow with thankfulness" (Colossians 2:6-7).

"And now, dear children, remain in fellowship with Christ so that when he returns, you will be full of courage and not shrink back from him in shame" (1 John 2:28).

_____

_____

_____

_____

_____

"I am the true grapevine, and my Father is the gardener. He cuts off every branch of mine that doesn't produce fruit, and he prunes the branches that do bear fruit so they will produce even more."
—Jesus
(John 15:1-2)

_____

_____

_____

_____

_____

"And this is his commandment: We must believe in the name of his Son, Jesus Christ, and love one another, just as he commanded us. Those who obey God's commandments remain in fellowship with him, and he with them. And we know he lives in us because the Spirit he gave us lives in us."
(1 John 3:23-24)

"This means that anyone who belongs to Christ has become a new person. The old life is gone; a new life has begun! And all of this is a gift from God, who brought us back to himself through Christ. And God has given us this task of reconciling people to him" (2 Corinthians 5:17-18).

"Those who say they live in God should live their lives as Jesus did" (1 John 2:6).

_____

_____

_____

_____

_____

_____

"You didn't choose me. I chose you. I appointed you to go and produce lasting fruit, so that the Father will give you whatever you ask for, using my name."
—Jesus
(John 15:16)

_____

_____

_____

_____

_____

Talk About It

During the last get-together, you were asked to consider what Jesus is doing in your life.

And depending on how you were feeling that day or what had happened lately, you might have sighed, "Not much."

But here's the thing: Sometimes you don't see what others see. You're too close, too in the moment to step back and see clearly.

So call or get together with someone who knows you well, and ask, "What have you seen Jesus doing in and through me lately?"

Listen carefully. It may be Jesus speaking to you through your friend.

And once you've listened to your friend, ask Jesus, "So what did you think about that?"

It Can Be Lonely at the Top

The leaders in your faith community are disciples, too, and they can always use encouragement. A thank-you note tucked under their windshield wipers. The occasional flower or scone appearing on their desks.

Your adventure: Decide what you'll do to encourage your faith community's leaders in the next seven days. It can be something simple (a heartfelt text) or something...less simple.

You and your group of four serenading a pastor one evening.

Or discovering a leader's favorite pizza and having it delivered.

Or writing chalk affirmations on a driveway while the leader's away from home.

It's up to you and Jesus. But do something positive, adventurous, and affirming.

Express the generosity that's growing in you as you're ever more connected to the heart of Jesus.

Quickly list pastors, youth leaders, Sunday school teachers, and other leaders in your faith community here:

_____

_____

_____

_____

_____

_____

_____

_____

Now jot down what you and Jesus think will bless and encourage one or more of those people:

_____

_____

_____

_____

_____

_____

_____

_____

_____

And when a person you bless thanks you, explain that it's all about the heart of Jesus. And then tell that leader about your experience with this *Friends of God Discipleship Adventure*!

You're a Friend of God—and Friends Share a Love That's Tender and Tough

If you want to know if someone's *really* your friend, ask her, "Do these jeans make my bottom look fat?"

An acquaintance will toss a yes or no in your direction without worrying much about how the answer affects you.

A casual friend will tell you whatever she thinks you want to hear.

But a *real* friend, a *true* friend, will pause, cast an appraising glance your way, and then answer the question carefully but honestly.

She'll speak the truth...in love.

That's what good friends do. And it's exactly what God does.

Friends don't shy away from truth-telling, but they don't use truth as a weapon. They let truth open doors without using it as a battering ram.

When you met with your discipleship group, you talked about times people have demonstrated tender as well as tough love. And you discovered that, ultimately, both flavors of love are still love.

Let's dig into that a bit further, seeing how God perfectly blends both tender and tough love in his friendship with us, with you.

But first, do these jeans...you know?

Okay, yeah. We thought so.

Thanks.

Jesus and the Pharisees

God is love, and Jesus reflects God's heart perfectly. Which means you can safely assume that Jesus perfectly loves every person he encounters—even if he's telling them they're wrong.

Take a look at these encounters between Jesus and the Pharisees, a group of religious leaders who were *way* more concerned with their rules than with the heart of God.

How is Jesus being loving in each of these encounters—and what do you think was the purpose of his love? Take notes—you'll be reporting back!

Disciples eat grain on the Sabbath (Matthew 12:1-8).

_____

_____

_____

Jesus heals a man with a deformed hand (Matthew 12:9-14).

_____

_____

_____

Jesus heals a man who's deaf and has a speech impediment (Mark 7:31-37).

Jesus is asked to show a miraculous sign (Matthew 12:38-45).

Jesus is asked about divorce (Matthew 19:1-12).

Jesus is asked if it's right to pay taxes to Caesar (Matthew 22:15-22).

Jesus warns the Pharisees (Matthew 23:23-28).

_____

_____

_____

Adventures in Discipleship

Before your next get-together with your discipleship group, embark on any or all of these discipleship-building adventures to help you experience God's love.

Loving Jesus When the Loving Gets Tough

We can't get enough of Jesus' tender love.

But what about when he confronts us about our addictions? Or when Jesus expects us to obey, no questions asked?

That's when some disciples turn away. It happened when Jesus was walking the earth, and it happens still.

But now that you've tasted a deepening friendship with Jesus, walking away won't be your story. Not even when Jesus loves you in a tough way.

Consider Peter, who was so concerned about Jesus' determination to go to Jerusalem, suffer, and die, that Peter took Jesus aside to straighten him out.

Jesus' response?

"Get away from me, Satan!"

Harsh words for a disciple to hear, words that might have caused another Jesus-follower to walk away.

But committed friends don't leave. They don't turn on their heel and storm off when they hear something they don't like. Instead, they stay and talk it through. They forgive what needs to be forgiven and understand what needs to be understood.

Peter stuck because that's what friends do.

The following Bible passages explore that kind of committed friendship. Read them with Jesus in mind, asking

"Why?" multiple times and pausing after each to invite Jesus to speak to you about what you've read.

Anything you hear, jot down.

Whether it's tender or tough.

> *"Another of his disciples said, 'Lord, first let me return home and bury my father.' But Jesus told him, 'Follow me now. Let the spiritually dead bury their own dead' "* (Mathew 8:21-22).

_____

_____

_____

_____

> *"If you love your father or mother more than you love me, you are not worthy of being mine; or if you love your son or daughter more than me, you are not worthy of being mine. If you refuse to take up your cross and follow me, you are not worthy of being mine. If you cling to your life, you will lose it; but if you give up your life for me, you will find it"* (Matthew 10:37-39).

_____

_____

_____

_____

"But I say, anyone who even looks at a woman with lust has already committed adultery with her in his heart. So if your eye—even your good eye—causes you to lust, gouge it out and throw it away. It is better for you to lose one part of your body than for your whole body to be thrown into hell."
(Matthew 5:28-29)

"If the world hates you, remember that it hated me first. The world would love you as one of its own if you belonged to it, but you are no longer part of the world. I chose you to come out of the world, so it hates you" (John 15:18-19).

"Then he said to the crowd, 'If any of you wants to be my follower, you must give up your own way, take up your cross daily, and follow me. If you try to hang on to your life, you will lose it. But if you give up your life for my sake, you will save it. And what do you benefit if you gain the whole world but are yourself lost or destroyed?'" (Luke 9:23-25).

"No one can serve two masters. For you will hate one and love the other; you will be devoted to one and despise the other. You cannot serve God and be enslaved to money. That is why I tell you not to worry about everyday life—whether you have enough food and drink, or enough clothes to wear. Isn't life more than food, and your body more than clothing?" (Matthew 6:24-25).

"I have loved you even as the Father has loved me. Remain in my love. When you obey my commandments, you remain in my love, just as I obey my Father's commandments and remain in his love" (John 15:9-10).

A Point to Ponder

G.K. Chesterton was a 19th-century Christian apologist who brilliantly captured the notion of Jesus' tender/tough love.

He wrote this: "If you meet the Jesus of the Gospels, you must redefine what love is, or you won't be able to stand him."

Read that quote aloud a few times, and then jot down your response to it:

Walking the Tightrope

Ephesians 4:15 describes one tension navigated by disciples: "Instead, we will speak the truth in love, growing in every way more and more like Christ, who is the head of his body, the church."

Speaking the truth in a loving way.

Loving in a truthful way.

Being both tender and tough.

Striking that balance is next to impossible, at least on your own. It takes the power of Jesus and generous nudges from the Holy Spirit to keep you from falling off that tightrope.

Briefly describe a situation in which you wish you'd been better able to speak the truth in a loving, constructive way. At home, work, school—anywhere.

Describe the situation in words or with a sketch—whatever helps you visualize the place and people involved.

When you've finished your description, ask Jesus, "How can I be truthful and loving in equal measure as I deal with this? What would you have me say or do—if anything?"

Ask...and then listen.

Because that's what disciples do.

When...I Feel

One way to speak the truth in love is to speak simply, clearly, and directly.

Especially when you're telling another person that you're not happy.

If you sometimes struggle with speaking up, or you tend to speak up in a way that tilts way more toward truth-telling than being loving, here's a handy tool to keep at the ready: "When...I Feel."

It's a quick formula that helps you communicate in a clear, respectful, and caring way. You're able to tell the truth as you see it minus any theatrics—and that's a good thing.

"When...I Feel" works like this: You simply state what's happening and how you feel about it. No accusations, no attacks, just reality from your point of view.

For instance, if someone ignores you in a meeting, you might say, "*When* you ignore me, *I feel* angry."

If someone mocks your faith, you might say, "*When* you make fun of me for trusting Jesus, *I feel* sad."

Notice: There's no manipulating, no quiet seething, just open, direct communication. You say your piece and then listen. If you've misread the other person, he or she will quickly correct you.

So do this: Thinking about the situation you described in the "Walking the Tightrope" section, write how you'd use the "When...I Feel" formula to respond to it by filling in the blanks below:

"When you_____,

I feel _____."

And now, while you're thinking about it, practice using this tool in other areas of conflict with co-workers, fellow students, neighbors, relatives—whoever:

"When you_____,
I feel _____."

"When you_____,
I feel _____."

"When you_____,
I feel _____."

"When you_____,
I feel _____."

"When you_____,
I feel _____."

"When you_____,
I feel _____."

"When you_____,
I feel _____."

"When you_____,
I feel _____."

"When you_____,
I feel _____."

"When you_____,
I feel _____."

Tuck this practical way to be a truth-teller in your pocket, and use it over the next few days when appropriate.

Then jot down how it went, and how you felt about those encounters:

_____

_____

_____

_____

_____

Talk About It

David, who wrote a sizable chunk of Psalms, did something remarkable: He invited God to be both tender and tough with him.

He wrote this: "Search me, O God, and know my heart; test me and know my anxious thoughts. Point out anything in me that offends you, and lead me along the path of everlasting life" (Psalm 139:23-24).

That invitation took courage. It leans into what friends of God do: trust that God wants only what's best for them, no matter how it feels at the moment.

You—you're a friend of God.

Are you willing to do what David did? Invite God inside, holding back nothing, welcoming the light he shines into the dark corners?

Read this aloud:

"Search me, O God, and know my heart; test me and know my anxious thoughts. Point out anything in me that offends you, and lead me along the path of everlasting life."

And now...listen.

See what your friend God might have to say to you.

You're a Friend of God—and Friends Trust One Another

Jesus said this to his first disciples: "If you cling to your life, you will lose it; but if you give up your life for me, you will find it" (Matthew 10:39).

Wow...that deal takes a *lot* of trust in Jesus.

Surrender the life you know for the promise of a better one? No wonder not everyone who meets Jesus takes him up on the offer.

But it's the deal we disciples get. We sign on to follow Jesus and to live out the same unreasonable commitment to him that he lives out for us.

We choose to trust him. And when we do, we discover he's completely trustworthy.

In this session, you'll focus on trusting Jesus—*really* trusting him. Trusting him as the friend he is: one who'll literally give his life for you.

That's the Jesus we're getting to know better as we see his heart for us.

And who wouldn't trust a friend like that?

Troubles and Hardships

Take a few minutes to list some of the challenges you're facing.

Friendship meltdowns, job problems, health issues—whatever comes to mind when you think: "This is a trouble or hardship for me right now..."

Stories About Jesus and Trust

Choose a passage from the list below:

1. **A father with a convulsing son** (Mark 9:16-25)
2. **Jesus, his disciples, Mary, Martha, and Lazarus** (John 11:1-44)
3. **Jesus, Jairus, and a suffering woman** (Luke 8:40-56)

Then discuss these questions:

- What are all the ways trust factors into this story?

- Why do you suppose the person or people in this encounter decided to trust Jesus?

- As you pay closer attention to this encounter, what builds your own trust in Jesus?

Adventures in Discipleship

 Before you meet again, dig into these discipleship-building adventures...

More Stories About Jesus and Trust

When you got together with your discipleship group, you explored one of the three stories about Jesus and trust.

Now explore the two you didn't examine...and check out a few more.

See how trust played a part in each encounter. What did these people see in Jesus that prompted them to trust him so completely? What convinced them that Jesus was who he said he was?

See what you discover about Jesus and his heart for others.

Once you've read an encounter several times, remembering to ask "Why?" as you read, answer these three questions:

- What are all the ways trust factors into this story?

- Why do you suppose the person or people in this encounter decided to trust Jesus?

- As you pay closer attention to this encounter, what builds your own trust in Jesus?

1. **A father with a convulsing son** (Mark 9:16-25)

2. **Jesus, his disciples, Mary, Martha, and Lazarus**
    (John 11:1-44)

3. **Jesus, Jairus, and a suffering woman** (Luke 8:40-56)

4. **Peter** (John 21:12-17)

5. **Two men walking to Emmaus** (Luke 24:13-31)

6. **A demon-possessed man** (Luke 8:26-32)

7. **The devil** (Matthew 4:1-11)

If Jesus Is a Friend, Shouldn't Life Be Easier?

If you're thinking that a friendship with Jesus insulates you and people you love from hardship, your relationship with him has probably been a disappointment. That's because he never said he'd make life easy for you.

If anything, he promised that following him would *create* tension, put you at cross purposes with the culture, and invite problems.

The disciple Paul said it this way: "Yes, and everyone who wants to live a godly life in Christ Jesus will suffer persecution" (2 Timothy 3:12).

Blunt.

And accurate.

So expect challenges. Anticipate hardships. And trust Jesus through all of them.

By the way, if you're wondering if there's anything Jesus *has* promised to do for you, the answer is yes.

Read on.

Jesus promises you life.

"Then Jesus said to his disciples, 'If any of you wants to be my follower, you must give up your own way, take up your cross, and follow me. If you try to hang on to your life, you will lose it. But if you give up your life for my sake, you will save it' " (Matthew 16:24-25).

Jesus promises you acceptance.

"However, those the Father has given me will come to me, and I will never reject them" (John 6:37).

Jesus promises to reward your faithfulness.

" 'Yes,' Jesus replied, 'and I assure you that everyone who has given up house or brothers or sisters or mother or father or children or property, for my sake and for the Good News, will receive now in return a hundred times as many houses, brothers, sisters, mothers, children, and property—along with persecution. And in the world to come that person will have eternal life. But many who are the greatest now will be least important then, and those who seem least important now will be the greatest then' " (Mark 10:29-31).

Jesus promises you joy.

"I have loved you even as the Father has loved me. Remain in my love. When you obey my commandments, you remain in my love, just as I obey my Father's commandments and remain in his love. I have told you these things so that you will be filled with my joy. Yes, your joy will overflow!" (John 15:9-11).

Jesus promises you forgiveness.

"But if we confess our sins to him, he is faithful and just to forgive us our sins and to cleanse us from all wickedness" (1 John 1:9).

Jesus promises you friendship.

"You are my friends if you do what I command. I no longer call you servants, because a servant does not know his master's business. Instead, I have called you friends, for everything that I learned from my Father I have made known to you" (John 15:14-15, NIV).

Do you trust Jesus to deliver on these promises? If you do, how does that change your perspective of the tough stuff in your life?

Go back and read your list of troubles and hardships. Picture holding all of that in one hand and Jesus' promise of life and friendship in the other.

How do they compare?

Talk About It

Invite a fellow disciple to walk around your neighborhood with you.

Ask Jesus to prompt you to stop and pray in front of a home you're passing. Once you've stopped, ask Jesus how to pray for the people in that home.

Don't forget to give Jesus the opportunity to prompt you to pause in front of your own homes, too.

When you and your friend have finished walking and praying, talk about this:

- How was this like or unlike how the two of you usually pray?

- How has this experience affected your trust in Jesus?

You're a Friend of God— and Friends Forgive

Forgiveness is the duct tape of friendship.

Without forgiveness, what's broken by a thoughtless word or angry outburst stays broken. Without it, there's no rebooting a fractured friendship, no clearing the air and moving on.

Without forgiveness, friends don't stay friends for long.

And without forgiveness, disciples don't stay free for long. That's because a lack of forgiveness—either refusing to give it or to ask for it—binds us and hobbles our ability to follow Jesus.

Unforgiveness saps our lives of joy.

It keeps us from shining God's love in difficult situations.

And it sets us up as blockades rather than bridges when it comes to sharing God's friendship with others.

Plus, there's this: Nothing draws us closer to God than forgiveness. We need his power to forgive...and we need to come to him for forgiveness.

Because, as we'll discover, forgiveness isn't something we can do on our own.

Adventures in Discipleship

Before you meet with your discipleship group again, embark on some or all of these discipleship-building adventures that will help you experience Jesus' heart for forgiveness.

Jesus and Forgiveness

For disciples, the importance of both giving and asking for forgiveness can't be overstated. It's a central theme in Jesus' teaching and a reflection of his heart for you.

Read the following Bible passages, and ask Jesus to help you see his heart in them for you, for others, for his world.

> *"Make allowance for each other's faults, and forgive anyone who offends you. Remember, the Lord forgave you, so you must forgive others."*
> (Colossians 3:13)

Where's Jesus' heart in this passage? What does he reveal about himself?

_____

_____

_____

_____

_____

"So watch yourselves! If another believer sins, rebuke that person; then if there is repentance, forgive. Even if that person wrongs you seven times a day and each time turns again and asks forgiveness, you must forgive" (Luke 17:3-4).

Where's Jesus' heart in this passage? What does he reveal about himself?

_____

_____

_____

_____

_____

"Finally, I confessed all my sins to you and stopped trying to hide my guilt. I said to myself, 'I will confess my rebellion to the Lord.' And you forgave me! All my guilt is gone" (Psalm 32:5).

Where's Jesus' heart in this passage? What does he reveal about himself?

_____

_____

_____

_____

_____

*"**Where is another God like you, who pardons the guilt of the remnant, overlooking the sins of his special people? You will not stay angry with your people forever, because you delight in showing unfailing love. Once again you will have compassion on us. You will trample our sins under your feet and throw them into the depths of the ocean!**"* (Micah 7:18-19).

Where's Jesus' heart in this passage? What does he reveal about himself?

_____

_____

_____

_____

_____

*"**But if we confess our sins to him, he is faithful and just to forgive us our sins and to cleanse us from all wickedness**"* (1 John 1:9).

Where's Jesus' heart in this passage? What does he reveal about himself?

_____

_____

_____

_____

"But the Lord our God is merciful and forgiving, even though we have rebelled against him."
(Daniel 9:9)

Where's Jesus' heart in this passage? What does he reveal about himself?

_____

_____

_____

_____

_____

"So if you are presenting a sacrifice at the altar in the Temple and you suddenly remember that someone has something against you, leave your sacrifice there at the altar. Go and be reconciled to that person. Then come and offer your sacrifice to God" (Matthew 5:23-24).

Where's Jesus' heart in this passage? What does he reveal about himself?

_____

_____

_____

_____

_____

A Point to Ponder

Jesus hangs on a cross, each breath an agony.

He's been beaten. Bloodied. Through bruised eyes, he sees what no one around him sees: 10,000 angels filling the sky above him, hands resting on the hilts of their fiery swords, ready to swoop to his rescue if he'll just give the word.

The angels rivet their attention on Jesus, willing him to give a sign—any sign at all—that he's done with the suffering, finished with the pain.

And then Jesus lifts his face and speaks—but not to summon help. Instead, he speaks of his torturers.

He chokes out, "Father, forgive them, for they don't know what they are doing" (Luke 23:34).

It's a miracle. A miracle of forgiveness.

In the space below, describe what—if anything—that miracle means to you.

How to Ask for Forgiveness

Most people—disciples included—aren't very good at asking for forgiveness.

Instead, they mutter something that's a sort-of, almost, not-really apology.

"I'm sorry you felt hurt," for instance.

Or "I guess I could have handled that better."

Those don't really count as asking for forgiveness.

Following is a five-step process for asking for forgiveness. It gets past pretense and communicates authentic repentance.

1. Be honestly remorseful—and express that remorse.

"I'm sorry" or "I hope you can forgive me" is a great start to the conversation. There's no need for tears or theatrics; what is needed are directness and honesty.

2. Be specific about what you did.

Name it. Describe it. Let the other person know you're fully aware of what you did or failed to do, what you said or failed to say.

3. If at all possible, make amends.

Fix what you broke. Replace what you took. There may be nothing you can do, but if there is, do it.

4. If there's an explanation for your actions, offer it.

Just make sure it's an honest explanation and comes with a promise that what happened won't happen again. This is not about excusing your behavior or blaming others. You did it—admit it.

5. Finally, actually ask for forgiveness.

Say these words aloud: "Please forgive me." Lay it on the line, and then wait until you get a response. The other person may not be ready to forgive you just yet, but you can ask.

Accepting Forgiveness

Here's something many disciples encounter: Though God is willing to forgive us for something we've done, we have a hard time forgiving ourselves.

We continue carrying guilt and shame even though there's no need to. We can't quite take God at his word that, if we confess, he'll set us free through his grace.

As a result, we slink around, not trusting God and waiting for a "Ha! Gotcha!" from on high. And we never experience the joy that comes from forgiveness.

Well, you're going to see if you can get past that with a little help from God...and a close friend.

Choose a friend you're confident can keep a secret, someone you're convinced loves you.

Tell that person there's something you want to get off your chest and you'd like help doing it. Arrange for a time to talk in a place you won't be overheard.

And when you meet, meet in person, not over the phone.

When you're with your friend, explain that you're discovering that forgiveness is a lifestyle. That forgiveness is freeing. And that, as you've examined your life, you realize some of the unforgiveness you carry around is directed at yourself.

Tell your friend you've decided to confess something you can't forgive yourself for even though you believe God has forgiven you.

Your friend's part is to listen as you talk and to keep listening until you've got it all out. Until you've brought what you've been hiding into the light.

Tell your friend her job isn't to make excuses for your behavior. Or to tell you it's no big deal. Because it *is* a big deal; it's a roadblock in your friendship with God.

When you've finished, when you've said what you've been afraid to say for so long, your friend will do this: Read aloud 1 John 1:8-9...more than once.

Let the truth of that passage sweep away your guilt and self-loathing. Let Jesus use those words to erase your shame.

Sit in silence with your friend—with *both* your friends. Jesus hasn't left you—he's not ashamed to be with you. It's time you weren't ashamed to be with yourself.

Thank your friend—both your friends—and then let go. That's what forgiveness feels like.

"If we claim we have no sin, we are only fooling ourselves and not living in the truth. But if we confess our sins to him, he is faithful and just to forgive us our sins and to cleanse us from all wickedness."

(1 John 1:8-9)

Forgiving Someone Else

Head to the dollar store and buy a helium balloon. Take a permanent marker with you, or pick one up while you're balloon shopping.

The balloon's design doesn't matter, but get one that's colorful and easy to see.

Take your balloon to an open field or parking lot—somewhere your view isn't blocked by trees or buildings.

Using the marker, write something you've found hard to forgive on the balloon. Be specific, but don't name names.

Invite Jesus to join you as you release the balloon. Ask him to stand beside you as the two of you watch it grow smaller, then smaller still, and then disappear altogether.

As you watch, ask Jesus this question: "How can you help the pain I feel about what I wrote fade away, just as the balloon is fading into the distance?"

Listen carefully. The answer may be hard to hear, but it will bring healing.

When you get home, write about this experience. What, if anything, did Jesus reveal to you? How might Jesus come alongside you to help you forgive others?

_____

_____

_____

_____

_____

_____

_____

_____

_____

_____

_____

_____

This experience is adapted from _Growing Spiritual Grit_ from Group Publishing.

Next Steps

What? You thought you were graduating?

Disciples *never* graduate—they keep growing closer to Jesus and are always open to inviting others to enjoy a friendship with Jesus, too.

You're shining the light of God's love—and Jesus has placed you in the perfect spot to shine it brightly into your friendships.

Jesus said this to his first disciples:

"You are the light of the world—like a city on a hilltop that cannot be hidden. No one lights a lamp and then puts it under a basket. Instead, a lamp is placed on a stand, where it gives light to everyone in the house. In the same way, let your good deeds shine out for all to see, so that everyone will praise your heavenly Father."

(Matthew 5:14-16)

So a question for you: What's next, disciple?

In your discipleship group, you asked Jesus that question, and we'd like to suggest this: Be open to sharing with others what you've received in this discipleship experience. If it was helpful to you, it'll be helpful to others you know.

You can share in several ways...

- **Stay connected to the disciples you've met.**

Do the five bonus adventures described in the following pages together, and then circle back to experience this entire adventure again. It won't feel repetitive; you've grown and are entering from a new place. You can go deeper.

- **Invite new people to enjoy this discipleship experience with you.**

You've launched spiritual conversations with friends outside of the group get-togethers; ask those people if they'd also like to go on this discipleship adventure. Whether they're long-time Christians, new believers, or not-yet-believers, God is eager to have them as friends.

Help their friendship with God grow.

It's easy to get additional diaries and leadership materials. Contact your local Christian bookstore or visit Group Publishing at **group.com** for details.

- **Attend or launch a Lifetree Café®.**

Lifetree Café® is created by the same people who crafted this discipleship experience, and for the same reason: to draw people closer to Jesus. Weekly conversations about fascinating topics and people provide a real-world opportunity to strengthen your ability to share, listen, and exercise other discipleship skills. Visit **LifetreeCafe.com** for more information and to discover the Lifetree Café closest to you.

- **Serve through Lifetree Adventures®.**

You can serve locally and globally through Lifetree Adventures' unique discipleship-building programs that blend service with spiritual growth. It's double-time discipleship that gives you a great chance to grow. Check out **LifetreeAdventures.com** to see where you might go.

Whatever you're led to do, keep growing. Keep abiding. Keep following Jesus.

You're a disciple...and that's what disciples do.

Bonus Adventure 1: Embrace Humility

This will be fun.

Buy a bottle of bubbles—the kind that comes with a wand.

Recruit a friend to sit with you on a park bench and take turns blowing bubbles. Lots of bubbles. Offer passersby opportunities to give it a try, too, especially people who look like they could use some cheering up.

And little kids. Little kids *love* bubbles.

Run that bottle right down until there's nothing but fumes in it.

Then talk about this with your friend:

- How was having the humility to have fun like this in public good for you...and challenging for you? What does it remind you of elsewhere in your life?

- Humility is often cited as a necessary ingredient in following Jesus. How has that been true for you—or hasn't it?

- Tell about a time you saw humility in action. Who was humble—and what happened?

- Together, ask Jesus to help you see opportunities to be humble. And if you're *really* brave, ask Jesus to humble you.

Bonus Adventure 2: Pay Attention to Jesus

It's field trip time.

Take another Jesus-follower with you on this adventure—and make sure you'll have time to talk about it when it's over.

Go to the nearest hospital emergency room, and when you get to the door, pray this: "Jesus, for the next hour, we're at your disposal. You lead, and we'll follow."

Then walk in, find seats in the waiting area, and trust that Jesus will tell you what's next.

Maybe he'll ask you to pray for that woman weeping in the corner. Or to strike up a conversation with the angry man pacing the room.

Trust Jesus for direction. For the right words. For whatever's coming next.

After you're out the door, talk about this:

- What was challenging or easy about this experience?

- What did you discover about yourself and each other through this experience?

- In what ways did putting yourself out there without a plan build your trust in Jesus?

- Tell about a time you heard from Jesus in an unmistakable way. What was the situation, and what did you do? Or hasn't that happened for you?

- Ask Jesus to help you see and hear him.

Bonus Adventure 3:
Serve Without Being Thanked

Find some heavy-duty trash bags and work gloves.

All set?

Good—you and your friend are about to spend a few hours serving people who aren't likely to thank you.

Some won't notice what you're doing.

Others will notice but not care.

Either way, don't count on anyone appreciating you as you stroll through your neighborhoods picking up trash on sidewalks, blown into doorways, or otherwise landed where nobody's likely to clean it up.

Some things for you and your friend to talk about as you fill your bags with broken glass, discarded cans, and stray scraps of who-knows-what:

- How does it feel to serve when nobody appreciates you or your efforts?

- In what ways is that like or unlike what Jesus expects from his disciples?

- If you could nominate someone you know for Servant of the Year, who would you choose, and why?

- Tell about a time someone served you and you didn't appreciate it until much later, if ever.

- Thank Jesus for serving you—and be specific.

Bonus Adventure 4:
Catch Yourself Judging Others

Find a spot that's good for people-watching.

A public park. The zoo. A bench at the mall.

Then do this: You and your friend decide which people you're drawn to and which you aren't. Two lists—people you'd welcome if they were to sit down next to you and those who, as far as you're concerned, can keep on walking.

Mentally sort passersby for 10 or 15 minutes, comparing notes as you go.

And be honest. No posturing here; don't describe how you think you should judge others. Describe how you *actually* judge others.

Because no matter how uncomfortable the thought, you *do* judge others. We all do.

Then you and your friend talk about this:

- What did you discover about how you judge others?

- What sort of picture did your comments paint? Is it a portrait of people who are caring? curious? open—or closed?

- How comfortable are you with others judging you in the same way you've judged them?

- Tell about a time you judged someone and, for better or worse, you were right. Who was it, and what was the situation?

- Tell about a time you judged someone and then discovered you were dead wrong about the person. What happened? How did you feel?

- Ask Jesus how he'd have you judge—or not judge—others. What does he have to say about that?

Bonus Adventure 5: Take a Stand

Ask another disciple to help you select a business or organization the two of you think doesn't honor Jesus.

Maybe it's a strip club. Or a government office. Or a massage parlor that offers more than massages.

Together, go to that place and stand near it.

Be legal—stand on a sidewalk or other public access area. And there's no need for bullhorns, bombast, or signs. You're there to pray, not preach.

Pray that everyone in that organization's circle of influence will discover what you've discovered: God wants to be their friend.

That's it. That's all.

Because it's enough.

When someone discovers the transforming power of God's friendship, everything changes.

When you've finished praying, talk about this:

• How does taking a stand for Jesus feel?

• Do you think it counts to take a stand so quietly? Why or why not?

• How much confidence do you have that your prayers will make any difference? Why?

• Tell about a time you overtly took a stand for Jesus. What was the situation, and how did it turn out? Or haven't you done that yet?

• Together, ask Jesus to give you the courage to publicly identify with him. Ask how he might want that to happen.

These five bonus adventures are adapted from *Growing Spiritual Grit for Teenagers* from Group Publishing.

Notes

Notes

Notes

Notes

Notes